The First Battle of the Marne: The History and Legacy Allied Victory in World War I

By Charles River Editors

A picture of British soldiers at the battle

About Charles River Editors

Charles River Editors is a boutique digital publishing company, specializing in bringing history back to life with educational and engaging books on a wide range of topics. Keep up to date with our new and free offerings with this 5 second sign up on our weekly mailing list, and visit Our Kindle Author Page to see other recently published Kindle titles.

We make these books for you and always want to know our readers' opinions, so we encourage you to leave reviews and look forward to publishing new and exciting titles each week.

Introduction

A picture of French soldiers advancing during the battle

The First Battle of the Marne

"So we come to the Marne. This will ever remain the Mystery Battle of all time. We can see more clearly across the mists of time how Hannibal conquered at Cannea, than why Joffre won at the Marne. No great acquisition of strength to either side - except that usually invaders outrun their supplies and defenders fall back upon their reserves - important, but not decisive. Not much real fighting, comparatively few casualties, no decisive episode in any part of the immense field; fifty explanations, all well documented, five hundred volumes of narrative and comment - but the mystery remains." – Winston Churchill

World War I, also known in its time as the "Great War" or the "War to End all Wars", was an unprecedented holocaust in terms of its sheer scale. Fought by men who hailed from all corners of the globe, it saw millions of soldiers do battle in brutal assaults of attrition which dragged on for months with little to no respite. Tens of millions of artillery shells and untold hundreds of millions of rifle and machine gun bullets were fired in a conflict that demonstrated man's capacity to kill each other on a heretofore unprecedented scale, and as always, such a war brought about technological innovation at a rate that made the boom of the Industrial Revolution seem stagnant.

The enduring image of World War I is of men stuck in muddy trenches, and of vast armies deadlocked in a fight neither could win. It was a war of barbed wire, poison gas, and horrific losses as officers led their troops on mass charges across No Man's Land and into a hail of bullets. While these impressions are all too true, they hide the fact that trench warfare was dynamic and constantly evolving throughout the war as all armies struggled to find a way to break through the opposing lines.

Though World War I is almost synonymous with trench warfare, that method of combat was nothing new. There had been extensive use of trenches during the later stages of the American Civil War (1864-1865), and trench warfare was constant during the Second Boer War (1899-1902), the Russo-Japanese War (1904-1905), and the Balkan Wars (1912-1913). These conflicts showed that modern firepower combined with entrenched positions gave a decisive advantage to the defender, yet European observers failed to learn any lessons from these conflicts, and the scale of trench warfare in World War I far eclipsed anything seen before or since, especially on the Western Front.

Since the Industrial Revolution, arms and materiel output had increased by orders of magnitude, as had the quality and uniformity of the products. Several developments had already taken place in the years building up to the conflict, stepping stones towards the vast escalation in military innovation which took place immediately prior to and during World War I. Chief among these was the invention of smokeless gunpowder, which took place concurrently among several powers between 1890 and 1905. This was a crucial development, as it eliminated the literal "fog of war" which in vast quantities obscured the battlefield entirely and on an individual level both gave away the position of marksmen and made it impossible for them to fire accurately unless they moved away from their own smoke-cloud. Further innovations included the adoption into service of the first belt-fed machine guns, predecessors of those which would wreak such slaughter in the trenches, and the development of cannon which did not roll backwards after each shot as 19th century pieces did, but remained fixed in place.

The arms race before the war and the attempt to break the deadlock of the Western and Eastern Fronts by any means possible changed the face of battle in ways that would have previously been deemed unthinkable. Before 1914, flying machines were objects of public curiosity; the first flights of any account on rotor aircraft had been made less than 5 years before and were considered to be the province of daredevils and lunatics. By 1918, all the great powers were fielding squadrons of fighting aircraft armed with machine guns and bombs, to say nothing of light reconnaissance planes. Tanks, a common feature on the battlefield by 1918, had not previously existed outside of the realm of science fiction stories written by authors like H.G. Wells. Machine guns had gone from being heavy, cumbersome pieces with elaborate water-cooling systems to single-man-portable, magazine-fed affairs like the Chauchat, the Lewis Gun and the M1918 BAR. To these grim innovations were added flamethrowers, hand grenades, zeppelins, observation balloons, poison gas, and other improvements or inventions that revolutionized the face of warfare.

These technological developments led to an imbalance. Before the introduction of the man-portable light machine gun (which took place in the second half of the war), not to mention tanks (which also joined the fight late in the game), defensive firepower vastly outweighed offensive capability. Massed batteries of artillery, emplaced heavy machine guns, barbed wire entanglements, and bewildering fortifications meant that ground could not be taken except at incredible cost. This led to the (somewhat unjustified) criticism famously leveled at the generals of World War I that their soldiers were "lions led by donkeys". Certainly, every army that fought in the Great War had its share of officers, at all levels of command, who were incompetent, unsuitable, foolish, or just plain stupid, but there were plenty of seasoned professionals who understood their job and did it well. The main problem facing commanders in the war was that there was such a bewildering array of new armaments, with such vast destructive potential, that previous military doctrines were virtually useless. Cavalry, which had been expected to play a major role both as reconnaissance and as "mounted infantry", operating in much the same way as airborne and mechanized troops would later to rapidly outflank enemy positions, quickly proved useless. Frontal infantry assaults were cut to shreds by enemy defensive fire, but there seemed to be no major alternative. Ground had to be taken, even if at great cost, and to do so, more destructive weapons were devised, tested and deployed.

Needless to say, the First World War came at an unfortunate time for those who would fight in it. After an initial period of relatively rapid maneuver during which the German forces pushing through Belgium and the French and British forces attempting to stymie them made an endless series of abortive flanking movements that extended the lines to the sea, a stalemate naturally tended to develop. The infamous trench lines soon snaked across the French and Belgian countryside, creating an essentially futile static slaughterhouse whose sinister memory remains to this day.

If trench warfare was an inevitability during the war, it is only because the events leading up to the First Battle of the Marne were quite different. The armies at the beginning of the war moved quickly through the land, but the First Battle of the Marne devolved into a bloody pitched battle that led to the construction of trenches after the Germans retreated, blocked in their pursuit of Paris. When the aftermath disintegrated into a war between trenches, some Germans thought they had the upper hand since they were occupying French territory, but with fewer soldiers than the combined Allied nations and fewer resources and supplies, it was possibly only a matter of time before they were ultimately defeated. The commander of the German armies, General Helmuth von Moltke, allegedly said to Kaiser Wilhelm II immediately after the First Battle of the Marne, "Your Majesty, we have lost the war." Winston Churchill himself would later reference that anecdote, writing, "Whether General von Moltke actually said to the Emperor, 'Majesty, we have lost the war,' we do not know. We know anyhow that with a prescience greater in political than in military affairs, he wrote to his wife on the night of the 9th, 'Things have not gone well. The fighting east of Paris has not gone in our favour, and we shall have to pay for the damage we have done.'"

The First Battle of the Marne: The History and Legacy of the First Major Allied Victory in World War I analyzes one of the Great War's most important conflicts, and how it brought about trench warfare. Along with pictures of important people, places, and events, you will learn about the First Battle of the Marne like never before.

The First Battle of the Marne: The History and Legacy of the First Major Allied Victory in World War I

About Charles River Editors

Introduction

    The Start of the War

    The Invasion of Belgium

    The Battle of the Frontiers

    Things Go Awry for the Germans

    The First Battle of the Marne

    The Race to the Sea

    The Aftermath of the Marne

    The Legacy of the Battle

    Pictures of the Battle

    Online Resources

    Bibliography

Free Books by Charles River Editors

Discounted Books by Charles River Editors

The Start of the War

"You will be home before the leaves have fallen from the trees." - Kaiser Wilhelm II, August 1914

By the 20th century, warfare was nothing new to the European powers, especially when it came to fighting each other. Conflicts had been a mainstay on the European continent for over two millennia. Even after the Napoleonic wars had enveloped Europe in large scale war for nearly 20 years in the 19th century, the Europeans' imperialism continued unabated. It would take the devastation of World War I to shock Europe and jolt the world's superpowers out of their imperialistic tendencies.

After Napoleon and the French were was finally defeated in 1815 by a coalition of European nations, Europe went about their most serious attempt to create peace on the continent. Even before the fighting had ended, most major European powers had been meeting in Vienna and established a congress in 1814. A series of agreements were reached between the coalition and the defeated French to end the fighting.

However, the Europeans continued to conduct business as usual, spending much of the 19th century engaged in imperialism across the world. The natural response of the European nations was to establish alliances that would maintain at least a balance of power. In 1873, German chancellor Otto van Bismarck reached an alliance with Austria-Hungary's despot and the Russian czar. The French signed alliances with Britain and Russia, who had left its previous alliance over tension brought about by Austria-Hungary's intervention in the Balkans. By then, Italy had joined the German alliance.

Although a couple of wars were fought on the European continent during the 19th century, an uneasy peace was mostly maintained across the continent for most of the 19th century after Napoleon. Despite this ostensible peace, the Europeans were steadily conducting arms races against each other, particularly Germany and Britain. Britain had been the world's foremost naval power for centuries, but Germany hoped to build its way to naval supremacy. The rest of Europe joined in on the arms race in the decade before the war started.

With Europe anticipating a potential war, all that was missing was a conflagration. That would start in 1908, when Austria-Hungary annexed Bosnia-Herzegovina in the Balkan Peninsula, drawing it into dispute with Russia. Moreover, this upset neighboring Serbia, which was an independent nation. From 1912-1913, a conflict was fought in the Balkans between the Balkan League and the Ottoman Empire, resulting in the weakening of the Ottoman Turks. After the First Balkan War, a second was fought months later between members of the Balkan League itself.

The final straw came June 28, 1914, when a Serbian assassinated Archduke Franz Ferdinand, the heir to the throne of Austria-Hungary, in Sarajevo, Bosnia. The world reacted with horror to the death of Franz Ferdinand and Sophie, nowhere more so than throughout Austria-Hungary, where there was widespread rioting against innocent Serbian citizens living within the empire's borders. It is surmised that many of those displaced eventually made their way back across the border to Serbia as refugees, further inflaming sentiment against Austrians and making an already volatile situation that much worse. Expressions of horror and commiseration came in from Germany, France, Britain (although the public and the government's attention there were far more focused on the rapidly escalating crisis in Ireland, where the independence movement had turned violent), and even Austria's recent enemy, Italy. Russia also offered its condolences, which was quite hypocritical given that the Russian government was almost certainly aware of the Serbian plot.

Overwhelmingly, the Great Powers sided with Austria, and a joint Austro-Hungarian and German demand was presented to the Serbian government to commence an internal investigation into the assassination, but the Serbian Ministry of Foreign Affairs dismissed such a request out of hand, claiming that there was absolutely nothing to investigate. This further aggravated an already awkward situation.

In the wake of the investigation into the death of Franz Ferdinand and the resulting trial and sentences that followed, along with the verdict of the court inculpating Serbia for the murders, the Austro-Hungarian Empire ultimately issued a letter to Serbia which became known as the July Ultimatum. This inflammatory letter demanded that the Kingdom of Serbia repudiate in writing the acts of the terrorists intent on destabilizing the legitimacy of the Austro-Hungarian monarchy and their hold over Bosnia-Herzegovina, and it also reminded the Serbian government that it had bound itself to abide by the terms of the agreement ceding it to Austria-Hungary in the first place. The letter also listed 10 key points which Serbia was expected to accept within 48 hours, and it threatened retaliation in the case of non-compliance.

The points listed were as follows:

1. Serbia must renounce all propaganda designed to inspire hatred towards Austria-Hungary and which might prove harmful to its territorial integrity.

2. The Organization known as the People's Defence must be disbanded forthwith, along with all organizations of a similar ilk.

3. All propaganda against Austria-Hungary published in public documents, including school textbooks, is to be eliminated forthwith.

4. All officers and government officials named by the Austro-Hungarian government are to be removed from office immediately.

5. Members of the Austro-Hungarian government will be dispatched immediately to Belgrade, where they are to be given every assistance in suppressing subversive movements.

6. All those involved in Franz Ferdinand's assassination are to be brought to trial forthwith, with the assistance of police investigators from Austria-Hungary.

7. Major Vojislav Tankosic and Milan Ciganovic, known participants in the assassination of the royal couple, are to be immediately arrested.

8. The Serbian government must cease all collusion in the transportation of weapons and equipment across the Austro-Hungarian Border, dismissing and disciplining the Border Patrol officials at Sabac and Loznica, who abetted the Sarajevo conspirators.

9. Provide suitable explanation to the Austro-Hungarian government with regards to the actions undertaken by certain Serbian officials, who have demonstrated an attitude of hostility in their negotiations with the Austrian government.

10. Immediately notify the Austro-Hungarian government once these measures have been enacted.

The letter set off a frantic flurry of activity in Serbia, but not of the kind the Austro-Hungarians wanted, aside from those in office who were clearly spoiling for a fight. Serbia telegraphed to St Petersburg asking for support, which Russia promised in the event of a fight. Reassured, Serbia then mobilized its armed forces before sending a reply to the July Ultimatum that conceded both points 8 and 10 but rejected the remaining points. The Serbs disguised their explicit refusal with a wealth of diplomatic actions that did nothing to fool the Austro-Hungarian government. The response from the empire was swift; the Austro-Hungarian ambassador in Belgrade was recalled, and troops began to prepare in for mobilization.

A propaganda cartoon after the assassination that asserted "Serbia must die!"

The day after the Austro-Hungarian ambassador departed from Belgrade, a convoy of Serbian troops being transported down the Danube River by steamer drifted off course towards the Austro-Hungarian bank near Temes-Kubin, where the local garrison commander ordered shots fired into the air to discourage them from landing. He wisely avoided firing upon the boats, which might well have precipitated a full-scale crisis, but as it was, his level-headedness would be to no avail. Unfortunately, the report which reached Emperor Franz Joseph I in Vienna about this incident inaccurately portrayed the trifling affair as a bloody last-ditch skirmish, and Franz Joseph I responded by declaring war. The Austrian Army was brought forward to a state of full mobilization, and the allotted divisions moved forward to their position on the Serbian border.

This was the move that set the dominoes of war in motion. Russia and France immediately mobilized their armies in response to the Austro-Hungarian threat, as they were required to do so according to the terms of the Secret Treaty of 1892, which stated that any mobilization of members of the Triple Alliance must be met. The initial, limited mobilization by Austria-Hungary was followed by a full-scale Russian one, which in turn was followed by a full-scale German and Austro-Hungarian call-up, which in turn precipitated a French one and finally a British one. Thus, with a suddenness that startled even those who felt it was inevitable, the major European powers all found themselves at war.

Although there had been explicit displays of commiseration and sympathy for Austria and widespread condemnation of Serbia's actions in the immediate aftermath of Franz Ferdinand's assassination, the attitude of the great powers towards Austria as the notional aggrieved party became substantially chillier as Austria insisted on virtually bullying Serbia over the whole affair. The British Prime Minister, Asquith, complained in an official letter that Serbia had no hope of appeasing Austria diplomatically, and that the terms of the July Ultimatum would've been impossible to meet even if Serbia was willing to do so. Indeed, it appears as though such an exacting document had been drafted precisely because Serbia didn't have a hope of complying, even if they had so wished, and thus Austria-Hungary would be able to go to war and punish them properly for the outrage perpetrated against their royal family.

100 years removed from the assassination, it might be unfair to say that it caused World War I, but it certainly started it. Historians still debate whether the Great War would have occurred even if Franz Ferdinand and Sophie lived out their lives in peace and comfort, but many believe that while it might've come months or years down the road, it was inevitable. The tangled web of alliances at cross-purposes, the growing diplomatic tensions, the arms race, the belligerence of newly powerful states such as Germany, the interference in other sovereign countries' affairs, and the relentless politicking all pointed towards one tragic outcome.

As for the parties themselves, it's apparent that much of the blame can be shouldered by the Serbian government. To this day, it's still unclear how much the King and Prime Minister knew about the plots and actions carried out by Dimitrijević and his associates in the Black Hand, but they were obviously privy to the official communications that involved Dimitrijević in his capacity as the head of Serbian Military Intelligence. Furthermore, it was the Serbian government, not the Black Hand (which at that point was virtually synonymous with Dimitrijević and Military Intelligence in any case) that provided Princip, Grabež, Cubrilovic, and the other conspirators with their firearms, explosives, training, and the means to cross the border into Bosnia. The People's Defence, the clandestine group within Bosnia, had been almost completely taken over by Serbian Military Intelligence and was effectively acting as a shell organization. Government officials from several different agencies had colluded with the conspirators on many occasions, with the end result that on the day of the assassination, the assassins were in place, suitably organized, well-armed for their purpose, and ready for action. At the same time, there are strong indications that several officials within the Serbian government (with or without sanction from on high) attempted to warn their Austro-Hungarian counterparts of what was to come.

Another country that must bear a share of the blame is Russia. According to the confession given by Dimitrijević at the end of his 1917 trial in Salonika, Russia was fully aware of his activities, and he had no reason to lie at that point. Indeed, according to Dimitrijević, the Russian Military Attachè in Belgrade had guaranteed that Russia would stand with Serbia against Austria-Hungary in the event that the operation was compromised, and that he had received funds from Russia to carry out the assassination. An investigative journalist attempting to uncover the truth received a fairly unconvincing testimony from the Russian Military Attachè, who denied any involvement. The Russian Military Attachè claimed that his Assistant had been in charge during the period leading up to the assassination, and that Dimitrijević never apprised him of his plans or intentions. It has also been suggested that the Tsar, or at the very least the Prime Minister, were aware of a forthcoming attempt against Franz Ferdinand's life and were not opposed to it happening. Russia had a vested interest both in weakening the Austro-Hungarian Empire and in destabilizing its hold on the Balkans as this might well potentially give it access to the strategically invaluable Mediterranean ports without having to pass through the Turkish-controlled Bosphorus and Dardanelles straits, which hampered its attempts to increase its naval power outside of the Black Sea.

Even Austria-Hungary, despite being the aggrieved party, had a hand in what followed the assassination. The Austro-Hungarian military had resisted many attempts at pacification with Serbia, including policies advocated by Franz Ferdinand himself, and it continued to pursue a policy of aggressive saber-rattling. Furthermore, the Governor of Bosnia, Oskar Potiorek, was a rigid and stubborn individual who viewed Slavic patriots as a national security threat and ruthlessly punished them accordingly, further inflaming anti-Austrian sentiment in a newly created province that required the most delicate of management rather than hamfisted pacification attempts. His refusal to countenance the use of improperly dressed troops to shield Franz Ferdinand and his halting of the motorcade in a vulnerable position near the bank of the river were symptomatic of his stubbornness, and his decision to remain idle while Sarajevo tore apart the homes of hundreds of innocent Serbs is evidence of his poor character.

Ironically, one of the few people who had no blame in what was to come was Franz Ferdinand himself. A choleric individual with the typical Austrian aristocrat's condescending attitude towards the subordinate Hungarian population, he was nonetheless no more prejudiced than many during his time and a great deal less than most; after all, he married a woman from the Czech aristocracy who was beneath his station. On top of that, his attitude towards Serbia and the Slavic issue was remarkably conciliatory for someone in his position. He went to his death unwittingly even after bravely continuing his public appearance despite having a hand grenade hurled at him. It is unfortunate for Franz Ferdinand that his birth and position made him an ideal target, but as history and fate would have it, he was simply the right man in the wrong place at the wrong time.

The Invasion of Belgium

When World War I began in August 1914, all armies envisioned a war of movement that would lead to a quick victory. Cavalry units little changed since the Napoleonic era would act as scouts, skirmishers, and as a screen for the main army, and coming behind these would be masses of infantry with relatively few machine guns and field artillery as support. There was little in the way of aerial reconnaissance, and radio communication was in its infancy, to the extent that radio transmissions were often sent in the clear with no attempt at encryption. This was especially true of Russian communications, but all armies were guilty of this in the early days. Thus, while it could be easy to find out enemy dispositions, it remained difficult to communicate this to friendly units in the field. Armies often moved blind, or with only the vaguest idea of the disposition of enemy troops.

For all sides at the start, the emphasis was on attack. Little thought was given to defensive systems except by Belgium, which was a neutral nation and relied on a massive system of forts to delay any invader long enough for guarantors such as the United Kingdom to come to its aid. As it turned out, this was exactly what happened.

Although details of Alfred von Schlieffen's plans were destroyed in World War II when the building holding the archives was bombed by the Allies, it seems clear von Schlieffen had gone into quite a bit of detail. He had outlined exactly what divisions would be deployed in each army and also gave the left flank more soldiers than the right, He envisioned his plan like a hammer that was coming down right on top of the French army, which would be trapped in the region of Alsace-Lorraine.

Von Schlieffen

The Schlieffen Plan had the 1st Army on the far west, the 2nd Army next to it to the east, the 3rd Army further east, and then the 4th Army next to that one. These armies were to move straight ahead until they had reached a mid-point between the border and Paris. Then they were to make an almost 90 degree turn to the east and arrive near Paris in a line from east to west. Beyond them, further east, the 5th, 6th, and 7th Armies would move in and take positions. The basic idea was that the 1st-5th Armies would come in and trap the majority of the French armies, which would be caught between them and the 6th-7th Armies.

Although the Schlieffen Plan was militarily elegant, it had several flaws which would turn out to be fatal. For one thing, the plans required constant movement, seeking to avoid a war with dug-in positions because that would slow down an advance. It allowed commanders of each army to make their own decisions, but at the same time these commanders had to stick to the basic plan and timetable. It did not have ways of dealing with the fog of war or unforeseen circumstances, and the plan required good communication, which was not possible at this point with existing technology. Moreover, von Schlieffen had not properly taken into account the problems with supplying the troops as the supply lines became stretched by the time the armies approached Paris. Finally, it misjudged a wide range of delaying tactics the French and the Belgians would use to slow down the Germans' forward movement.

If the plan had been implemented just as von Schlieffen designed it in 1905, it may have succeeded, but instead, the principal general 10 years later, General Helmuth Moltke the Younger, Chief of the German General Staff, kept modifying it to the point that the basic structure of the plan was significantly weaker. As historian T.M. Holmes put it, "If we want to visualize Schlieffen's stated principles for the conduct of a two front war coming to fruition under the circumstances of 1914, what we get in the first place is the image of a gigantic *Kesselschlacht* to pulverize the French army on German soil, the very antithesis of Moltke's disastrous lunge deep into France. That radical break with Schlieffen's strategic thinking ruined the chance of an early victory in the west on which the Germans had pinned all their hopes of prevailing in a two-front war."

On August 3 Germany declared war on Russia's ally, France, and a day later, at 5:00 a.m. on August 4, the German armies invaded Belgium. The Germans announced the supposed justifications for their actions: "Part of the speech made today in the Reichstag by the Imperial Chancellor [ED: of Germany] on the subject of the infamous violation of Belgian neutrality:-- "We are in a state of legitimate defence, and necessity knows no law. Our troops have occupied Luxemburg and have perhaps already entered Belgium. This is contrary to the dictates of international law. France has, it is true, declared at Brussels that she was prepared to respect the neutrality of Belgium so long as it was respected by her adversary. But we knew that France was ready to invade Belgium. France could wait; we could not. A French attack upon our flank in the region of the Lower Rhine might have been fatal. We were, therefore, compelled to ride roughshod over the legitimate protests of the Governments of Luxemburg and Belgium. For the wrong which we are thus doing, we will make reparation as soon as our military object is attained"[1] Ironically, it seemed the French were willing to invade Belgium themselves if needed, but since this never came to pass, France was able to appear more moral and upstanding in fighting the Germans.

When war broke out, the Germans did not have an alternate plan, so they felt somewhat beholden to the Schlieffen Plan and therefore had to move quickly once armies began to mobilize. Since the Schlieffen Plan depended on a precise timetable, it was the mobilization of the Russian armed forces that started the clock ticking as far as the Germans were concerned. According to the plan, they only had six weeks to subdue France before they had to face Russia in the east, which meant the Germans had to secure victory by mid-September at the latest. Put simply, there was no time to lose.

The Germans were acutely aware that the Allies, at this point consisting primarily of France, Britain, and Russia, were collectively more powerful and had more resources. The Schlieffen Plan aimed to ensure that Germany did not try to fight all of these nations at the same time, but even at this early stage, Germany had made a number of major miscalculations. The Germans were unsure whether an invasion of Belgium would compel the British to declare war, but sure enough, the British did so the very day the German invasion of Belgium commenced. 120,000 professional soldiers of the British Expeditionary Force (BEF) landed in France to help the French on August 7, just three days after the British declaration of war.

It also turned out that the Russians were able to mobilize much faster than the German plans assumed, and this was particularly troublesome for the Germans since their entire timetable was based on the Russians taking more time to get ready.

There was even more bad news, and it was the most immediate. The Germans expected the Belgians to either be easily defeated or to surrender without a fight, but this did not happen. In fact, the Belgian resistance became a major thorn in the side of the Germans and created delays they had not counted on. On top of all that, the Belgians tore up railroad tracks and blew up bridges which further slowed the German advance.

The Battle of Liège in Belgium is considered the first battle of the war. The town of Liège was protected by a large modern circular fortress that was designed to protect the town, and Liège also had a crucial juncture of railroads. The new German large howitzers, known as Big Berthas, were able to systematically pulverize the fortress, but the Belgian resistance there still managed

---

[1] Baron Beyens (Belgian Minister at Berlin). "Speech in the Reichstag by the Imperial Chancellor on the violation of Belgian neutrality." The Belgian Grey Book, August 4, 1914, https://wwi.lib.byu.edu/index.php/The_Belgian_Grey_Book.

to slow down the German advance by about five days. It would be one of the deciding factors that led to the German defeat at the First Battle of the Marne about three weeks later.

A Big Bertha

While the Germans turned out to be overly optimistic about their abilities and the time it would take to win, the French mistakenly assumed it would take the Germans a week or 10 days before their reserves were fully mobilized. In reality, the Germans accomplished that feat in little more than a day, which meant a much bigger German army was ready and able to take on the French more quickly than anticipated. At the same time, the French at this point in the war did not know about the Schlieffen Plan and the timetable the Germans were trying to meet.

Both sides quickly realized they had miscalculated the strength of the forts. The Belgians thought they would hold out longer than they did, while the Germans thought they would fall more quickly. The Germans believed they could reduce the forts in only a couple of days, but the defenders managed to hold out for 10 days. In the end, Belgium lost 90% of its territory in the opening weeks of the war, but the German timetable for the invasion of France was thrown into disarray.

This offensive spirit was seen in other ways. Troops were not supplied with steel helmets to protect them while firing from entrenched positions, and there was a marked shortage in barbed wire, shovels, and other equipment necessary for digging in and fighting from trenches. In fact, generals emphasized the idea of constant attack so much that in some of the opening battles, French commanders ordered their men to remove the bolts from their rifles and take German positions at the point of the bayonet. This reliance on *élan* made for good newspaper headlines, but exchanging a modern army for a medieval one led to horrible casualties, and the practice was soon stopped by even the most starry-eyed commanders.

A picture of French soldiers charging with bayonets

The Battle of the Frontiers

"The French army… accepts no law in the conduct of operations other than the offensive… only the offensive yields positive results… Battles are above all moral contests. Defeat is inevitable when the hope of victory ceases. Success comes, not to the side that has suffered the fewer losses, but to the side whose will is the steadiest and whose morale is the most highly tempered."2 - Field regulations of October 1913, influenced by Commander-In-Chief General Joseph Joffre

The Battle of the Frontiers is the name given to a series of battles along the French border as German armies invaded the country. In each case, when the French attacked, they suffered terrible losses and were thrown back into retreat. Taken together, these battles were the largest in history up to that time, involving an estimated 2 million men and producing more casualties than any battle before it. It was a grim demonstration that the war, thanks to the advances in technology and mass production, would wreak more destruction than ever before.

---

2 Allwood, Greg. "Deliverance On The Marne." Forces.Net, 5th September 2017, https://www.forces.net/news/deliverance-marne.

On August 22, 27,000 French soldiers were killed in the worst single day for the French Army. These casualties were incurred in five separate confrontations along the frontier, spread across the landscape from Belgium to Lorraine.3

In the fighting, the French casualties were so high because they did not yet appreciate the advantages of defensive positions, instead relying on old school ideals that their superior élan would carry the day. The Germans were fully aware of the French military philosophy and the reliance on fighting offensively, so one of the German techniques from the start was to advance and then hunker down into a defensive position, welcoming the French to attack. When the French did so, their soldiers were slaughtered by machine guns and accurate artillery, allowing the Germans to decimate the enemy while they dug in and protected themselves.

Most of these battles lasted no longer than a few days, and in most of them, the massive force of the German armies simply brushed the French armies aside and let the Germans continue on their way, just as the Schlieffen Plan had designed.

The Battle of Alsace, fought from August 7-10, was the first attack by French forces to reclaim Alsace. They succeeded at first but then were counterattacked. The battle ended in a stalemate, but the French withdrew due to terrible losses in other battles along the frontier.

The Battle of the Ardennes was fought from August 21-23 as the German 4th and 5th Armies invaded France at the Belgian-French border. The French were soundly beaten and forced to retreat. Soldiers from this battle were part of what came to be known as the Great Retreat.

In the Battle of Charleroi, fought from August 21–23, the French armies attempted to stop the 2nd and 3rd German armies from invading France at the Belgian town of Charleroi. They were completely defeated and suffered huge casualties. The French soldiers were almost captured, but they managed to escape and join the Great Retreat.

At the Battle of Mons on August 23, British soldiers held the German 1st Army in check and inflicted many casualties, but they were also eventually forced to join the Great Retreat.

General Joseph Joffre was the Commander-in-Chief of the French armies, and it was his strategy of attack that was responsible for the high number of casualties in the Battle of the Frontiers. Nevertheless, he was able to orchestrate an orderly retreat, and as he rallied and reorganized his soldiers close to Paris, his leadership would prove crucial for what took place at the Marne.

While no Allied commander knew exactly what the Germans were doing, they knew enough to

---

3 Trouillard, Stéphanie (August 22, 2014). "August 22, 1914: The bloodiest day in French military history". France 24, 22/08/2014, https://www.france24.com/en/20140822-august-22-1914-battle-frontiers-bloodiest-day-french-military-history.

get out of the way when faced with overwhelming force, which is what Joffre finally did after his attacks failed. He ordered a general retreat to the south and east, and while a retreat can often represent a humiliating loss, it can also be another military maneuver which if executed properly can put an army or armies into a much better fighting position. This is what Joffre knew he had to do.

Joffre

The Great Retreat occurred in an orderly enough manner that the Allied forces managed to avoid having their equipment captured over the course of about 10 days. It also gave the Germans the illusion they had essentially won the war, although General Moltke warned his men that the lack of prisoners and the inability to capture resources suggested the French armies were not only still intact but also disciplined and cooperating.

Things Go Awry for the Germans

While the Battle of Lorraine is considered part of the Battle of the Frontiers, it was actually quite different in nature because it represented French aggression separate of the German advance. The French wanted to reclaim the land known as Alsace-Lorraine from the Germans, who had taken the territory during the Franco-Prussian War about 40 years earlier.

In this regard, the French had their own master plan, not unlike the Schlieffen Plan, known as Plan XVII. Pursuant to this, the French would cross the German Lorraine border and go into the former regions of Alsace and Lorraine to free them from German domination. Feelings ran high when it came to Alsace-Lorraine, not only because it represented both a humiliating defeat but also because the French felt they had been robbed of a resourceful area they had always considered to be part of France.

A poster with text by Victor Hugo that means, "This sky is our shade of blue and this field is our land! This Lorraine and this Alsace, it's ours!"4

---

4 " 'Ce ciel est notre azur ce champ est notre terre! Cette Lorraine et cette Alsace, c'est á nous!'

In fact, von Schlieffen was counting on French emotions to play a part in the eventual French defeat, so when General Joseph Joffre crossed the German border into Lorraine, he was falling into the trap von Schlieffen had set for him. The strategy was for the German soldiers to put up stiff resistance but gradually fall back, tricking the French into believing they had a victory. Then, toward the end of August and the beginning of September, massive German armies would arrive from the west and attack the French from behind. At this point, the other German armies that had fallen back would attack from the other direction. This was called the *Hammerschlag* ("Hammer Blow") by the Germans, an indication they expected the French army to be hammered by the western German armies onto the anvil of the eastern German armies. That would spell the end of the French.

For this to work, von Schlieffen wanted the French troops to be in the open in Alsace-Lorraine so they could be squeezed and defeated, but he also did not want them anywhere near the extensive French fortifications along the French border, which would be very hard to attack and would bog the German armies down into a drawn out battle. These French defensive positions were particularly troublesome to the Germans, which is why they chose to go through Belgium in the first place.

There was only one problem, though it did not seem like a problem at first. That problem was Rupprecht, Crown Prince of Bavaria, who was in charge of the 6th German army facing the attacking French. While it's not clear exactly why things went the way they did, it seems likely that Rupprecht, who was still fairly young at the age of 43, wanted his share of the glory before the Germans finished off the French.

Victor Hugo" 3f03941v.jpg. Library of Congress Prints and Photographs Division Washington, D.C., 1918, http://www.loc.gov/pictures/item/99613754/.

Rupprecht

After considerable pressure, General von Moltke was talked into allowing Rupprecht's army to attack and pursue the French, so the Battle of Lorraine went on much longer than other battles at the borders. Indeed, it lasted until the French had been pushed back to their starting positions on August 25, which should have been a clear warning to General von Moltke because that attack on the French did not fit with the Schlieffen Plan. Nevertheless, Rupprecht's 6th Army and the 7th German army adjacent to them now believed they had a chance to bag the entire French army.

While it might have seemed plausible, there was also a good chance the French would successfully make it back to their forts and hold off the Germans indefinitely, which was the exact opposite of what the Schlieffen Plan was designed to do.

As a result, the next battle was the Battle of the Trouée de Charmes, which took place in a gap between two fortresses where the Germans felt they could avoid the hardened defenses of the forts and break through to destroy the French army. The prize was tempting, and if successful it would have eliminated a French army and put the 6th and 7th German armies in a good position for attacks on other French armies.

However, the Germans did not realize the gap had been intentionally left there by French defense planners for a reason. As it turned out, the gap contained commanding high points that made the defensive positions formidable, and when the Germans attacked on August 26, they fell into a trap that led to their decimation. As Maurice Barrès put it, "If Paris was saved at the Marne, it was because Castelnau won at Rozelieures."[5]

The Battle of Grand Couronné, which took place between September 4 and September 13, was named after the fortress and region the French retreated after the Battle of Lorraine. Over the course of those days, the French, now safely inside their fortifications, managed to tie up two German armies that could have been more useful elsewhere. Thanks to the strength of the defensive positions, Joffre was able to leave a relatively small number of troops to defend the fort and move the rest of his troops via the extensive French rail system near the Marne, allowing them to participate in that decisive battle.

As historians have pointed out, the Germans, who had thus far been quite successful, allowed a military operation to occur in the very place they expressly intended to avoid. In fact, they had invaded Belgium to avoid the very fortifications two of their armies were now attacking, and when the First Battle of the Marne would start, the French and British troops would be exactly where von Schlieffen did not want them instead of being trapped between German armies at Alsace-Lorraine.

---

[5] Barrès, Maurice. *The Faith of France*. Paris, Houghton Mifflin & Company, 1918.

The First Battle of the Marne

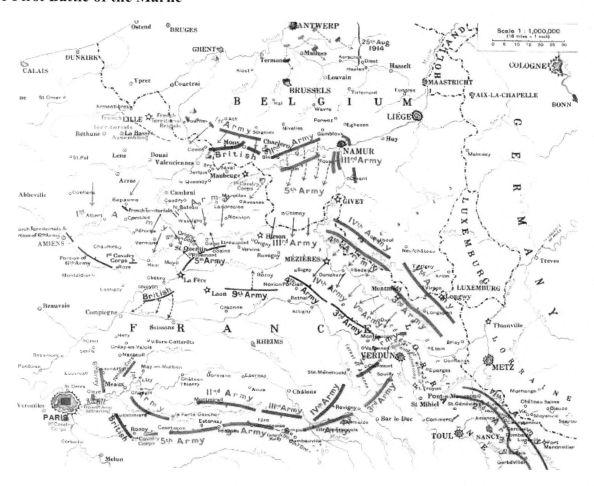

A map of the Allied armies and German armies outside of Paris

"At the moment when the battle upon which hangs the fate of France is about to begin, all must remember that the time for looking back is past; every effort must be concentrated on attacking and throwing the enemy back." – Joffre, September 5

Although it turned out the Germans had made a critical mistake, nobody could have known it when the First Battle of the Marne began on September 5. That battle, which would involve over 2 million soldiers spread out over a distance of 300 miles, was about to become one of the largest battles ever fought, but even then, the French were making contingency plans to evacuate their capital. General Joseph Gallieni, the Military Governor of Paris, made the following announcement:

"Abandonment of Paris

"The members of the Government of the Republic have left Paris, to give a fresh impulse to national defense.

"I have been intrusted with the task of defending Paris against the invader. That task I will fulfill to the end."

Gallieni

On September 4, the combined German armies closed in on Paris. Five German armies were in a line just north and east of Paris, but French armies still blocked the path about 20 miles away from the heart of the capital. Based on the Schlieffen Plan's timetable of six weeks to achieve total victory, the Germans at this point had about two weeks to conquer Paris, which certainly seemed manageable given the victories they had accrued over the previous month. In fact, the French did not disagree with this assessment – the government had fled Paris and moved to Bordeaux, taking the gold from the capital's Central Bank on the way out. By September 2, posters throughout the city told readers, "The members of the government of the Republic have left Paris to give a new impulse to the national defense."6

On August 26, the government had made a major decision by appointing Gallieni the new Military Governor of Paris, which meant he would be in command of the Paris Garrison and thus

---

6 Fierro, Alfred. Historical dictionary of Paris (1998, p. 216

wield the actual power in the city. This ancient title had its roots in the Middle Ages, but Gallieni's leadership would prove to be crucial in the First Battle of the Marne.

General Gallieni was hard-nosed, realistic, and decisive. He prepared for the worst and hoped for the best. Instead of being overly optimistic, he accepted the possibility that Paris might be taken by the Germans as they had during the Franco-Prussian War and thus rigged all the major Paris bridges with explosives. Gallieni had plans to wreck the sewers if necessary, and even the Eiffel Tower was set to be demolished since it could presumably be used for radio communications.

Gallieni was quite sure the Germans would reach Paris by September 5 if nothing was done, so he also prepared plans for the evacuation of Paris by civilians. Thing seemed so dire that many in Paris wanted him to declare it an "open city," meaning the Parisians would not put up any resistance and simply let the Germans march in and take over to avoid the destruction of their beloved capital. On September 2, German planes dropped leaflets onto Paris' streets with a s

However, as all of this was going on, Gallieni was also working on a plan to defeat the Germans, or at least prevent them from taking the city. He was kept abreast of the latest information on German troop movements and even studied aerial reconnaissance photographs. Airplanes were quite new. The Wright Brothers' first flight had only occurred 11 years earlier, so planes were still primitive, but Gallieni also understood the advantages they represented so long as the pilots knew what to look for while up in the air. The French had the most advanced and best developed aerial reconnaissance in the world at the time.

To Gallieni's astonishment, the French pilots seemed to bring him the miracle he had been hoping for, though aerial photography in 1914 was hard to understand for the uninitiated so it took some persuasion to convince others they had been delivered a hope. According to the pilots and the photographs, on September 3 a gap opened up between the westernmost army of the Germans, the 1st Army, and the 2nd Army, which the 1st Army had been ordered to protect. Days earlier, General Alexander von Kluck's 1st Army looked like it was going to attack Paris, but then it shifted to the southeast, apparently hoping to destroy the retreating French 5th Army.

Von Kluck

General Gallieni had to convince Joffre this gap existed, and then they had to agree on what to do, but unfortunately, Joffre and Gallieni had known each other before the war and their relationship had been strained. Gallieni had been Joffre's superior in the past, and now that Joffre was in charge, Gallieni was quite forceful in making his views known. On September 4, Gallieni called Joffre to inform him of the intelligence and his ideas, but Joffre refused to come to the phone and Gallieni would talk to no one else. As a result, Gallieni communicated with Joffre through aides, who relayed Gallieni's messages to the commanding general. Gallieni would later say, "The real Battle of the Marne was fought on the telephone."

In spite of their personal differences, the two came to an agreement and respected the judgment of the other. Gallieni had been put in command of the French 6th Army, created by Joffre just a few days earlier from the various battalions that had retreated from Lorraine and other places. That he was able to do this so quickly and create an organized army unit was quite remarkable in itself, and just as impressively, Gallieni immediately went ahead and ordered the 6th Army to attack the German First Army. He hoped to prevent them from trying to threaten Paris, and he wanted to force them to face the French attackers, which might open up the gap between the 1st

Army and 2nd Army even further.

Ahead of the fighting, German soldiers at the front and officials back in Berlin were extremely optimistic, which was somewhat understandable given the successes of the previous few weeks. When General von Kluck of the 1st Army was quoted as saying he would be in Paris in a week, the German Counsul-General Horst Flack laughed and said, "A week? I'll be you dollars to doughnuts that he'll march down the Champs Elysees in less than four days."

German soldiers may have been confident at the beginning of September, but General Moltke was more sober in his appraisal. Ahead of the battle, he noted, "We have hardly any horses left in the Army which can take another step. We don't want to fool ourselves – we've had successes, but we're not victorious yet. Victory means annihilation of the enemy's resistance, but where are all the French prisoners and guns which should have been captured? The French have retreated in a disciplined way according to a plan. The most difficult time lies ahead of us."7

Ironically, General Moltke was making a clearer assessment far away from the front lines than those who were in the front, but he correctly cautioned his troops to not take victory for granted and to not be surprised if the Allied forces were more substantial than they thought. Indeed, the five German armies would be facing six French armies and the British Expeditionary Force at the Marne, and for Moltke, the lack of prisoners and guns meant the Allies had lived to fight another day and were on their home turf. As it turned out, the numerical advantage had shifted in favor of the Allies, who had 56 divisions confronting 44 German divisions outside of Paris. Moreover, Rupprecht and his army remained occupied with a small number of French soldiers safely ensconced in fortifications.

Shortly before the fighting started, Joffre issued the following orders:

"General Instructions 5:

1. Advantage must be taken of the adventurous situation of the I German Army (right wing) to concentrate upon it the efforts of the Allied armies of the extreme left. All dispositions will be taken during the 5th of September with a view to commencing the attack on the 6th.

2. The dispositions to be realised by the evening of September 5 will be:

(a) All the available forces of the 6th Army, to the north-east, ready to cross the Ourcq between Lizy-sur-Ourcq and May-en-Multien, in the general direction of Château-Thierry. The available elements of the 1st Cavalry Corps that are in the vicinity will be put under the orders of General Maunoury for this operation.

---

7   Allwood, Greg. "Deliverance On The Marne." Forces.Net, 5th September 2017, https://www.forces.net/news/deliverance-marne.

(b) The British Army, established on the front Changis–Coulommiers, facing east, ready to attack in the general direction of Montmirail.

(c) The 5th Army, closing up slightly to the left, will establish itself on the general front Courtacon–Esternay–Sezanne, ready to attack in the general direction south to north, the 2nd Cavalry Corps assuring connection between the British and 5th Armies.

(d) The 9th Army will cover the right of the 5th Army, holding the southern end of the Marshes of St. Gond, and carrying a part of its forces on to the plateau to the north of Sezanne.

3. The offensive will be begun by these different armies in the morning of September 6."

(e) To the 4th Army: To-morrow, September 6, our armies of the left will attack in front and flank the I and II German armies. The 4th Army, stopping its southward movement, will oppose the enemy, combining its movement with that of the 3rd Army, which, debouching to the north of Revigny, will assume the offensive, moving westward.

(f) To the 3rd Army: The 3rd Army, covering itself on the north-east, will debouch westward to attack the left flank of the enemy forces, which are marching west of the Argonne. It will combine its action with that of the 4th Army, which has orders to attack the enemy."

The gist of this directive by Joffre was simple. The 6th French Army would attack the flank of the 1st German Army, the BEF would go through the gap between the 1st and 2nd German armies on the eastern side, and the French 5th Army would go through the gap on the western side of the German 2nd Army.

Meanwhile, the French armies needed to distract the German armies from realizing that they were being enveloped. Ferdinand Foch and the 9th Army would do their best to protect the flank of the 5th Army and basically keep the 3rd German army occupied, and French 3rd and 4th Armies keep the most eastern German 4th and 5th Armies occupied. As it turned out, Foch and others on the middle and eastern end of the German line would be pushed back, but the Germans would never able to break through.

Foch

Gallieni had soldiers from the Paris garrisons under his command, which included four territorial divisions, and he had also been given command of General Michel-Joseph Maunoury's newly formed 6th Army by Joffre, presumably to defend Paris. Other brigades (artillery, territorial, reserve infantry) were put at his disposal as well. These were all important, as they would later be ferried out to the front in the famous Taxis of the Marne in just a couple of days.

Late on September 5, Gallieni had ordered the 6th Army to move into position to face and then attack the German 1st Army. Since Paris was under a direct threat, Gallieni came to the conclusion that he needed to attack immediately with his own authority, and it was his orders to the 6th Army that started the advancing movement of Allied troops. Of course, the Allies assumed Paris was the immediate target for the Germans, and the Germans certainly wanted it to look that way, but according to some modern historians, the taking of Paris was considered secondary and not even desirable in the beginning. Instead, the German military aim was "the complete ruin of the enemy State by the destruction, the putting out of action, of its armies. Only an enemy completely disarmed will bow to the will of the conqueror... The opinion that prevailed with the German Staff is that to attack Paris before having finished with the Allied Armies would be a fault entailing very serious consequences..."

Thus, Gallieni, in assuming that Paris was the target, would actually open the door to capturing Paris by bringing the forces out of the city to attack the Germans. For their part, the Germans had changed their basic plan and decided to attempt encircling the Allied armies, the very same thing that the Allies were trying to do to them.

The German 1st Army had been chasing the retreating French 5th Army, which is why the German 1st Army was out of position at the start of the battle. In the German military culture, commanders were allowed great latitude when it came to their implementation of strategy and tactics as long as it did not jeopardize the overall plan, but in this case, General von Kluck had gone too far and did not realize it. "Numerically, the Germans were inferior to the Allies at the critical point, the right wing. Kluck's First Army of 128 battalions of infantry and 748 guns was ranged against 191 battalions and 942 guns of French Sixth Army and the BEF; Bülow's Second Army and half of Hausen's Third Army with 134 battalions and 844 guns faced 268 battalions and 1,084 guns of French Fifth and Ninth armies. It was a stark reversal from August 1914."

However, major mistakes were made by the French as well. The march of the French 6th Army to their position at the Ourcq River was detected early by General von Gronau of the German IV Reserve Corps. Von Gronau was responsible for protecting the extreme right flank of the 1st Army, and on the morning of September 5, he fired on the French 6th Army which meant that it was not able to get into its planned position. Making things worse, von Gronau was able to attack in the afternoon and push the 6th Army back into defensive positions, thus preventing them from positioning themselves for their planned assault. In the meantime, von Kluck, with time to spare, turned his army around to face the French 6th Army, which is not what the Allies or the French had planned on. They were expecting to face a smaller reserve army, not a massive professional army.

General Joseph Joffre sent out a message to be read to all his troops at the start of the battle: "At the moment when the battle upon which hangs the fate of France is about to begin, all must remember that the time for looking back is past; every effort must be concentrated on attacking and throwing the enemy back."

The Battle of the Ourcq, which began on September 5 and continued until September 9, is considered by many to be the first French military operation during the First Battle of the Marne. Named for the River Ourcq, the 6th Army led by General Maunoury attacked the most western German army on its western flank (the side closest to Paris), only to be forcefully pushed back by the Germans, who then threatened to approach Paris.

In response, on the night of September 7-8, Gallieni famously commandeered all the Paris taxicabs ("les taxis de la Marne") to take 6,000 soldiers directly to the battle, marking the first time automobiles had been used to take soldiers into combat. It significantly sped up the delivery of these men to the front lines where they were needed. Each cab took five soldiers (one in front and four in back), and they traveled at night, only turning on their tail lights for each cab to follow.

A picture of one of the cabs

While historians cannot agree whether this made a difference on the battlefield, the psychological benefit was enormous. The French, who had been retreating just out of reach of the Germans for almost two weeks, were now more energized and ready to fight back. In turn, their presence astonished the Germans, who did not expect the French to appear in such numbers.

In the middle of the Battle of the Ourcq, General Maunoury of the 6th French Army instigated a flamboyant raid designed to put the Germans on edge. Maunoury ordered General de Cornulier-Lucinière's 5th Cavalry Division to go behind German lines and create havoc, so on September 8, the division attacked an airfield which turned out to be important to the 1st Army. Just as he was attacking, General von Kluck and his aides showed up in automobiles by chance, but the German general and his entourage were able to defend themselves as they called in help. Soon the raiders were overwhelmed and had to retreat with a high number of casualties. In typical fashion, General von Kluck admired their spirit and called them the "brave raiders" who had just "missed a good prize."

Standing alone, the Battle of the Ourcq did not go well for the Allies, and though the French were not defeated, it compelled General von Kluck of the 1st Army to swing his huge force around to face the attacking French. When he did this, he opened the gap Gallieni had seen in reconnaissance photographs between the 1st and 2nd Armies even further. Now the gap was open so wide that the Allies could pour in between the two German armies and threaten both of them with encirclement.

Joffre still had one more task he had to accomplish: convincing General John French, the commander of the British Expeditionary Force, that the British needed to join the attack. Joffre knew the British were in just the right position to take advantage of the gap the next morning, but had no direct control over the British, so he counted on his powers of persuasion. He drove to French's headquarters and made a personal appeal, but things got a bit heated between the two leaders. According to reports, Joffre banged his fist on a table and exclaimed, "The honour of England is at stake!"[8] The liaison officer Lieutenant Edward Spears described the scene: "(Sir John French), who was awfully British and unemotive himself, was so moved (by Joffre's plea) that he struggled with the French language… he couldn't get anything out. And turning to somebody he said, 'tell him anything men can do, our men will do. We will attack tomorrow'."[9]

---

[8] Allwood, "Deliverance On The Marne."
[9] Allwood, "Deliverance On The Marne."

French

As luck would have it, the British would have the element of surprise because General von Kluck had written them off as an effective fighting ever since they commenced their retreat in Belgium. According to von Kluck, "The British have been beaten repeatedly and will scarcely be induced to come forward quickly and form a powerful offensive."10 Von Kluck's judgment could not have been further from the truth. When the British soldiers were told they were to attack, their spirits lifted. One of the British soldiers wrote, "The word began to filter down the line that we were on the move, in the reverse direction. At first, we found it difficult to believe. But sure enough, we soon found ourselves re-crossing the Marne and we were on the advance again… From being tired, worn out, demoralized creatures, we became what we were intended to be, trained soldiers with the enemy in view, and off we went." 11

As the Battle of the Ourcq continued in the far west between the French 6th Army and German

---

10 Allwood, "Deliverance On The Marne."
11 Allwood, "Deliverance On The Marne."

1st army, the next armies to the east were the BEF and the French 5th army, led by the flamboyant General Louis François d'Espèrey, who had written the original outline for the attack. As von Kluck wheeled his army to face the French 6th army, the gap between the German forces continued to widen, and the Allies pounced on September 6, with the British Expeditionary Force and the French 5th Army pouring through the divide. The 5th Army attacked the German 2nd Army, which was now in a delicate situation along with the 1st Army. The French caught the 2nd Army in a vulnerable position in a fight known as the Battle of the Two Morins, named after the two local rivers, the Grand Morin and the Petit Morin. The British, in turn, went beyond the Petit Morin, secured bridges that crossed the Marne, and secured a bridgehead five miles into German-held territory.

French forces fighting on the western side of the battle

In one of the horrific incidents of the war, the French showed that all sides could be responsible for atrocities. At nightfall, the German battalion dug some quick trenches and settled down for the night, not realizing where they were. The next morning, they discovered that French machine gun emplacements were positioned high up in a French farmhouse. Six machine guns opened fire on the trapped Germans, and the shooting did not stop even after the Germans put white flags on their bayonets and begged to surrender. Altogether, 450 German soldiers were killed and about 90 were taken prisoner in an episode that became known as the "Massacre of Guebarré Farm."

Despite these seeming successes, the BEF did not move fast enough for the French and fell short of their objectives. Although the BEF vastly outnumbered the Germans in the gap, General Haig of the BEF lost just seven men in three days and only advanced about 25 miles, leaving the French furious. Nevertheless, their presence on the east side of the 1st German army was critical because it signaled a possible encirclement.

The 1st Army was supposed to be protecting the right flank of the entire German line, and in particular protecting the 2nd Army right next to it. When it allowed the gap to open up between the two armies, many believe it was due to the relationship between the two armies' commanders. "General von Bülow… detested von Kluck and the feeling was certainly mutual. For a campaign in which close cooperation between the two armies was essential, this personal dislike was to have disastrous consequences. Von Bülow's caution and von Kluck's determination caused great problems once the war had begun. Von Bülow considered the defeat of the BEF (British Expeditionary Force) to be entirely a matter for von Kluck and he, therefore, ignored any reports of… British movements…as being irrelevant… Von Kluck, in turn, either ignored or disobeyed orders or requests which came from von Bülow."[12]

---

12 Lomas, David. *Mons 1914: The BEF's Tactical Triumph*. Bloomsbury USA, 09/15/1997.

Karl von Bülow

Even as the gap exposed the German 2nd Army, the 1st Army still held out hope it could defeat the French 6th Army. Meanwhile, the French began attacking the Third, Fourth, and Fifth Armies that were next in line to the 2nd Army. As this was going on, there was virtually no communication between the German armies in the field and their supreme commander, General Moltke, nor were the generals communicating with each other. On September 6 and 7, General Moltke did not give any orders, and for their part, von Kluck and von Bülow did not send reports to Moltke.

The German-occupied town of Marchais-en-Brie was subjected to a night bombardment on the evening of September 7. Such a bombardment was unusual at the time, and the next day the town was overrun by French troops. Next to Marchais-en-Brie was the important town of Montmirail, which could no longer be defended by the occupying Germans. General von Bülow, as a result, ordered his troops to pull back about 7 miles to the east, but in doing so made it impossible to close the breach between his army and the German 1st Army. The historian Sewell Tyng believes that this was the moment the battle was won, as it meant that the 1st Army was now isolated and the 2nd Army's flanks were open to attack. The 2nd Army now had the job of protecting the flank of the entire line of German armies, all of them were vulnerable.

Both the French and the Germans had now decided that their best chance of landing a knockout blow was to encircle one or more armies, which would then lead to the collapse of all the enemy armies. Incredibly, some historians believe this was truly possible for both sides, and that only a couple of days separated these outcomes.

As both sides blundered in the west, the situation further east was different. Foch's 9th Army was under attack by the German 3rd Army, and on paper, at least, it looked like the Germans might break through and pierce a hole directly in the center of the French line. Foch was in a most difficult position, one which he handled with grace and a clear head. It was his job to keep the German 3rd Army and some of the German 4th Army occupied so that the BEF and the French 5th Army could go through the gap on the west and outflank both the 1st and 2nd Armies.

Foch lost ground day after day as General von Hausen and the German 3rd Army pushed the French steadily back in hopes of breaking it. While von Bulow's 2nd Army was getting hammered at the Battle of the Two Morins by the French 5th Army, he urged General von Hausen to go after the French 9th Army in the vicinity of the Saint-Gond Marshes, an almost impenetrable area of wetlands. Foch was having a "gap" problem of his own at that time, as his 9th Army was about 10 miles from the French 4th Army and the Germans believed they could break through at that point.

Using simple logic, General von Hausen tried to pinpoint a position where the French were most vulnerable and came to the conclusion that it was the area of Foch's army right in front of his army. To win the battle, the Germans had to knock out the French artillery so his troops did not have to advance against their withering firepower, so he dramatically put together a plan to attack the French artillery positions under the cover of darkness with a bayonet charge. The soldiers were quite expert at handling bayonets and they could silently sneak up on the enemy without arousing suspicion. Once the French artillery was out of the way, von Hausen would have an open pathway for his soldiers to attack and break Foch's line.

At 2:15 a.m. on September 8, German soldiers of the 3rd Army were awakened and told to get ready. Half an hour later, the first attack started, and they were followed by another wave of

German soldiers at 3:00 a.m. and another at 3:30 a.m. The French were totally surprised, and by 6:00 a.m. things looked grim. The marshes had been outflanked, and his attempt to stem the tide of the German onslaught on his right wing failed. At this point, he told his army to pull back about 7 miles and appealed to Joffre and d'Espèrey to send him help. Unlike the poor cooperation between the Germans, both generals responded with more than Foch asked for, realizing the seriousness of the situation. The French center held, and with the help of Joffre and d'Espèrey, Foch was able to rectify the problems on the right before the Germans could take advantage.

At his headquarters back in Luxembourg, General von Moltke was beside himself. On September 7, he wrote to his wife, "Today a great decision will come about, since yesterday our entire army is fighting from Paris to Upper Alsace. Should I have to give my life today to bring about victory, I would do it gladly a thousand times...I often shudder when I think of this and I feel as though I need to accept responsibility for this dreadfulness." Feeling out of touch with the situation on the battlefield, Moltke decided he needed to know the situation firsthand, so he ordered a trusted aide, intelligence officer Richard Hentsch, to visit the headquarters of the 2nd Army and then the 1st Army.

On September 8, Gallieni cabled the French government, which had fled Paris and was now in Bordeaux, and asked them for assistance if Paris' residents needed to be evacuated. Gallieni was having second thoughts about his actions and was now afraid that his 6th Army might be beaten, leaving the door open to Paris. Since he had sent almost all of his soldiers to the front, Paris was virtually unprotected.

In doing this, he committed a major faux-pas, because by talking to the government directly, he had bypassed Joffre, who was understandably furious. Soon after that, Gallieni's post was placed within the military authority and the French army took over command of the 6th Army.

Later on September 8, Gallieni communicated with General Michel-Joseph Maunoury of the 6th Army. They agreed that the army was in no condition to launch an attack, but Gallieni insisted that they must hold their position and not open the way to Paris. Maunoury agreed that this was what he had to do, though his men were at the limit of their endurance. Gallieni knew the lay of the land well, so with his help Maunoury pulled back to a better defensive position.

Ironically, on that very same day, Hentsch conferred with General von Bülow, who believed his army was about to be encircled. Von Bülow wanted to pull back and Hentsch agreed, so he approved the general's plans. While many on the German side blame Hentsch for a hasty unqualified decision that led eventually to Germany's defeat four years later, Hentsch was cleared of any wrongdoing by a German military court that looked into the matter during the war. It appears he was well known to both the 1st and 2nd Army commanders, and that he knew his way around the battlefields of the Marne. Furthermore, the strategy of von Bulow, originally, was to only pull back a bit to the other side of the Marne. The following is the original argument as presented by von Bulow late in the evening to both his staff and Hentsch:

> "The II Army ...is no longer capable of forcing a decisive victory. As a result of the transfer of two army corps from the left to the right wing of the I Army, a gap has been created which forms an immediate danger to the inner wings of both the I and II Armies. I am informed that enemy columns, brigades or divisions, are on the march into this breach, and I have no reserves left to attack the enemy or to hold him off.
>
> "The enemy has two alternative courses open to him, either to turn against the left wing of the I Army or to march against the right wing of the II Army. Because of our lack of reserves, either movement might lead to a catastrophe. If the enemy compels a retreat by force of arms, the withdrawal would have to be made through a hostile country and the consequences to this Army might be incalculable. It should therefore be considered whether it would not be better, viewing the situation as a whole, to avert the danger by a voluntary concentric retreat of the I and II Armies."

As if to emphasize the point, right after von Bulow made this speech, his staff received a phone call that the town of Marchais-en-Brie had been taken by the French, which meant that the critical town of Montmirail that the Germans occupied could no longer be held. Given that von Bulow was immediately withdrawing another 7 miles or so, this seemed to solidify the belief that the 1st and 2nd Armies were too isolated and vulnerable.

While von Bülow began to retreat, Hentsch met with von Kluck the next day and told him to have the 1st Army retreat. Von Kluck initially refused - from their vantage point, they could see the top of the Eiffel Tower in Paris, and the German general still believed he was about to defeat the French 6th Army. Eventually, Hentsch pulled rank by asserting the authority of General Moltke and also pointed out the 2nd Army was retreating.

On September 10, Hentsch returned to Luxembourg to give General Moltke the sobering news. At that point, only the 1st and 2nd Armies were in retreat, and the High Command did not believe that the other armies at the Marne were in danger. Furthermore, they believed a general retreat would be terrible for morale.

On September 10, Crown Prince Wilhelm (the next in line to be Kaiser), who commanded the German 5th Army, decided to try one more time to overcome the French resistance. He planned another bayonet attack just as General von Hausen had done two days before, this time against the French 3rd Army on the western edge of the French line.

This time, however, the French were ready and waiting, and the outcome was a complete defeat for the Germans. The French's cannons decimated the 100,000 German soldiers, who became confused in the night and often tangled with each other. At 7:45 p.m., the French counter-attacked, and the carnage continued. Crown Prince Wilhelm would subsequently attempt to characterize this attack as a success, but by then Moltke realized that his commanders had been giving him exaggerated reports of their successes.

As the Germans were considering whether to withdraw all or only some of their armies, Foch forced their hand. On September 10 and 11, the 9th Army was able to repay the Germans with devastating attacks on the German Third Army. When this fighting was over, Foch had cost the German 3rd Army almost 15,000 more men, and by September 11, Joffre informed French War Minister Alexandre Millerand, "We have achieved a certain victory at the Battle of the Marne."

On September 11, Moltke, along with his staff and Hentsch, drove to the headquarters of the various commanders in the field. By the afternoon, they believed that the situation had stabilized, so they began drafting a communique to the 3rd, 4th, and 5th Armies instructing them to stay where they were. However, as they were doing this, a dire message from von Bulow was received, informing them that the 3rd Army was now being threatened by Foch's 9th Army. This was the last straw for Moltke, who then ordered all of his armies to retreat.

By the end of that night, all German armies were retreating to newly assigned positions. On September 12, von Kluck's 1st Army reached its new position above the Aisne River, but the gap between it and the 2nd Army still existed. Finally, on September 13, the two armies, with the help of German troops that had not fought at the Marne, closed the gap with little time to spare as the French and British were in hot pursuit.

When General Moltke realized his modified Schlieffen Plan had failed, he had a nervous breakdown, which required his subordinates to take over and oversee the massive pullback of the Germans to the River Aisne. While it seemed the Germans may have been too confident ahead of the First Battle of the Marne, the fact that the Germans quickly built formidable trenches on high ground after retreating about 40-50 miles to the Aisne makes clear that German planners had obviously considered this possibility. Indeed, these trenches were much better made, much better designed for defense, and more comfortable than those the Allies knew how to build early on in the war, and the Germans, more than the Allies, understood the power of a defensive position. Thus, the trenches were quite formidable despite the fact many Germans expected them to be temporary.

Near the very end of the First Battle of the Marne, it was the Allies who faltered. On

September 12, Joffre ordered his Third Army to outflank and prevent the German retreat, but it was to no avail. In the end, the Allies pursued the Germans too slowly, and by September 14, the Germans had established themselves on the high ground above the Aisne and secured that position. As Edward Spears, a liaison officer in the British Expeditionary Force, later explained, "I am deeply thankful that none of those who gazed across the Aisne of September 14 had the faintest glimmer of what was awaiting them."13

A photograph of the German trenches on the Aisne River after the German retreat from the First Battle of the Marne

The First Battle of the Aisne was the first battle of the war to feature trench warfare, and unfortunately for the Allies, the Germans had found the perfect defensive spot. On a high bluff overlooking the Aisne River, they had a commanding view, and on the other side of the river was a flat plain, making almost all enemy movements quite visible.

During this battle, the British tried to attack by crossing the river on boats at night and then use the morning fog as cover, but they were cut down in droves as the fog lifted. It almost immediately became obvious the German position was virtually impregnable, and General French recalled, "As day by day the trench fighting developed and I came to realise more and more the much greater relative power which modern weapons have given to the defence; as new

---

13 Klein,"The First Battle of the Marne."

methods were adopted in the defensive use of machine guns; and as unfamiliar weapons in the shape of 'trench mortars' and 'bombs,' hand grenades, etc. began to appear on the battlefield, so, day by day, I began dimly to apprehend what the future might have in store for us."[14]

When successive waves of British charges up the ridge were repulsed with heavy casualties and the German expertise at gunnery had become all too apparent, the British dug in as well. To either side of them, the French did the same, and the positions along the Aisne would be pretty much the same three years later.

---

[14] French, Field-Marshal John. *1914*. London, Constable And Company Ltd., 1919. French, 1914.

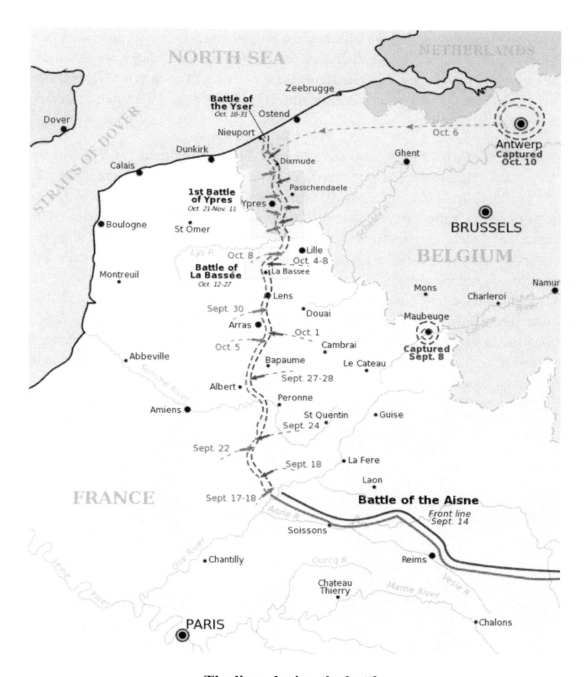

The lines during the battle

The Race to the Sea

When the assault across the Aisne ground to a halt, the French and British tried to outflank the Germans to the north, but they were stopped once again. Undeterred, they repeatedly tried to flank to the north in a frustrating series of battles lasting through mid-October that has been dubbed "The Race to the Sea." In the end, the opposing armies found themselves dug in from the Swiss border to the North Sea, a distance of about 475 miles. Trench warfare had begun in earnest.

The town of Ypres represented the westernmost Belgian town of any size and controlled a fairly important road and communications junction. It also lay in a shallow bowl formed by a series of low ridges rising some 160 feet above the surrounding flatlands at their highest point. These terrain features possessed considerable military value for the long-range observation they enabled over the countryside.

The deployment of Allied forces also had a bearing on the development of Ypres as a point of particularly bitter contests for much of the rest of the war. To the north, Belgian forces held the line to the nearby coast, and initially, the Belgian forces, led personally at times by their courageous monarch, King Albert I, attempted to counterattack the German advance. However, the Germans lured their less experienced adversaries into a trap at the village of Weerde, near Antwerp, and decimated one of their major assault columns. The American journalist Edward Alexander Powell described it vividly: "At 5:30 to the minute the whistles of the officers sounded shrilly and the mile-long line of men swept forward cheering. [...] Then, Hell itself broke loose. The whole German front, which for the past several hours had replied but feebly to the Belgian fire, spat a continuous stream of lead and flame. The rolling crash of musketry and the ripping snarl of machine guns were stabbed by the vicious *pom-pom-pom-pom-pom* of the quick-firers. [...] Back through the hedges, through the ditches, over the roadway came the Belgian infantry, crouching, stooping, running for their lives." (Essen, 1917, 225).

King Albert I

After this bloody reverse, the Belgians changed their strategy to stand fully on the defensive, and they even broke the coastal dikes to flood the terrain in front of their positions with the waters of the North Sea. This effectively blocked the Germans from advancing anywhere north of Ypres, though it also freed German forces for use elsewhere.

Furthermore, Ypres created a salient in the line – a projecting lobe that formed the most advanced Allied position for many years and represented the final scrap of unoccupied Belgium – made it a focus for offensives by both sides. The British Expeditionary Force (BEF) deployed precisely at the Ypres salient. Field Marshal Sir Douglas Haig and Sir John French convinced themselves that a decisive breakthrough at Ypres remained possible with just another "slight push," despite constant overwhelming proof that it was not. As a result, the British command's aggression inevitably channeled itself into these few square miles of land, and the French, whose lines stretched south from Ypres, also participated in the fighting there.

Those few miles of forward projection encouraged the fond delusions of the British leaders that it offered a jumping-off point for crashing through decisively to Antwerp and then into Germany. The Germans, on the other hand, viewed it as a location where they might hope to pierce the Allied line and break through to Calais, cutting off the BEF from reinforcement and resupply as well as forcing the surrender of the Belgians. With the British and Belgians eliminated from the continent, the Germans could then mop up the French at their leisure, or so their planners anticipated.

Each side, therefore, imagined Ypres would be the breakthrough point where they could pierce the enemy lines and bring the approaching trench-bound stalemate – a situation none of the powers had expected or wanted – to a rapid close. Thus, each party ensured that no such dramatic breakthrough could occur by concentrating their offensive forces head to head at Ypres.

The Aftermath of the Marne

Early fighting made clear that neither side was prepared for fighting from trenches. While all had been trained in making simple trenches as temporary defenses before continuing an advance, no military commander had envisioned the massive trench systems that would develop during the war. It was apparent something had to be done, but the high commands continued with the same mistakes, thinking that more guns and more men were all that was needed to achieve a breakthrough. As a result, lower officers and men in the ranks started devising their own tactics to kill the enemy and stay alive.

The terrain through which the front cut was varied. Near the Flemish coast, the land was low and men digging down even two or three feet hit water. Further south in the Argonne, there was also a high water table. In both of these regions, as in most places on the line, the Germans had chosen to entrench on what little high ground there was, further adding to the misery of the Allies, who were forced to build "trenches" above ground with massive lines of sandbags, sometimes as thick as 20 feet at the base and 10 feet at the top. Along the rest of the line it was possible to dig a standard trench in the earth, but the fight against water and subsidence was a constant one, even in the mountains at the very southern end of the Western Front.

All trenches, whether above or below ground, were built along the same basic design. The front of the trench was called the parapet and was ideally 10 feet high, thereby allowing men to walk along the length of the trench without fear of snipers. In order to see and fire out, there was a firestep of earth or sometimes wood that ran along the length of the trench. The back of the trench was called the parado. Both the parapet and the parado were topped with sandbags and shored up with revetments of logs, iron rebars, and more sandbags. The French often used wattle of interlaced branches and wicker.

Allied troops in 1916

French soldiers in a trench during the Battle of Verdun

Parapets often had steps called "sortie steps" cut into them to make it quick and easy for troops to go "over the top". A series of "grasping posts" set into the parapet gave the soldier something to grab onto while holding his rifle in his other hand, and large quantities of short ladders could be used as well. It was best to have men coming out all along the line rather than bunching up at a few sally points.

Generally, trenches were built on a zigzag pattern. This kept an explosion in one section of the trench from spreading shrapnel along the line, and it also isolated any breakthrough and kept attackers from firing down the length of the trench. There were usually three lines of trenches; the first was called the firing line, the second the support trench, and the third the reserve trench.

In parts of the line there may be more support trenches, often adding up to as many as 10 lines. Trenches were connected by communication trenches, also dug in a zigzag pattern, and latrines, dressing stations for the wounded, kitchens, and other necessary depots would be located in the communication trench.

A barber working on a soldier in a French trench

The British dug trenches in a jagged series of right angles to make a pattern similar to the crenellations atop a castle wall, with a section of about 10 feet sticking forward called a fire bay. Perpendicular sections connected them to stretches set a little further back, and these were called traverses. The Germans also adopted this technique.

Of course, this describes an ideal trench, but conditions on the ground often dictated otherwise. Muddy conditions and bombardment led to subsidence, heavy rain flooded entire areas, forcing the men to create new communication trenches. Sandbags would tear or get blown apart and needed constant replacing. Exhausted men may dig a trench to nonstandard proportions, and if an enemy trench was taken the survivors of the assault would then have to turn the parado into a parapet and add a firestep.

Extending out from the front or firing line were saps, narrow trenches running 20-30 yards out into No Man's Land to a small bay (often just a shell crater) where two or three men would sit listening at night for enemy movement. A French soldier remembered hating this duty, calling "the little listening posts of dreadful memory. It is difficult to imagine the suffering of the sentries…How often did the absolute solitude provoke panic at the slightest movement of an animal in the grass, at the stirring of a branch in the moonlight?"

The men considered sentry duty to be the worst task, as they were always tired thanks to long hours of manual labor and insufficient sleep for weeks on end. To be made to stand for hours at night, peering over the parapet or walking the rounds of the same short bit of dark trench, must have played on both minds and nerves. While the vast majority would struggle to do their duty and keep heavy eyelids open, some couldn't help but fall asleep, and the punishment for sleeping on sentry duty was death. A good officer or NCO would stop and chat with his sentries, which helped morale and helped keep them awake. The famous British author Robert Graves said of sentry duty, "At night our sentries had orders to stand with their head and shoulders above the parapet…It implied greater vigilance and self-confidence in the sentry, and also put the top of his head above the level of the parapet. Enemy machine guns were trained on this level, and it would be safer to get hit in the chest or shoulders than in the forehead."

Sentry duty was rotated with fatigue duty, during which the men would repair trenches, bring up food and supplies, and perform other such necessary tasks. Some jobs, like repairing exposed trenches, had to be done under the cover of night in order to reduce the chances of snipers or aerial observers.

With the Race to the Sea over, both sides dug in and the war of positioning was afoot. Offensives aimed to gain strategic points such as high ground or important railways close behind enemy lines. They would try to push back enemy salients or expand their own. Gone were the big sweeping movements across large sections of the map, even though the Allies never gave up hope of making a breakthrough.

At first, the French and British tried to break through with ever larger assaults. These would be preceded by heavy artillery bombardments in the hope that it would cut the German wire and destroy frontline defenses, but it rarely accomplished either objective. The Germans made some assaults as well, especially counterattacks against Allied salients, but the Germans already enjoyed the luxury of occupying French and Belgian territory, so they saw less of a need to go on the offensive. Paris was not going to be taken, and victory could be obtained by simply holding on.

There were also sudden surprise attacks without artillery preparation, which would often come just after dawn or just before dusk. Since the Allied trenches faced east, the rising sun would be in the solders' eyes, and the same held true for the sunset on the Germans. Thus, both sides had orders to "stand to" at these times, meaning all available troops not on essential duty would stand on the firestep and await an enemy attack.

As casualties mounted, commanders began to experiment with different types of attack formation. The Germans had already been trained to charge in open order to reduce casualties from shrapnel and machine guns, and their opponents adopted this practice too. In the first winter of the war, the Germans tried various other methods to break through enemy trenches, such as night attacks focused at certain points. If the men broke into the enemy trench, they'd work their way along it, killing the enemy as they went. Another technique was to bring machine guns and snipers close to the enemy trench and clear them with heavy fire, and by the end of 1915 both sides were making liberal use of grenades, with special parties of grenadiers, to clear out enemy trenches.

Picture of German soldiers charging in an open formation

Not surprisingly, snipers proved their importance in this new war of position. While most of the armies didn't have specialized snipers in 1914, those who had been marksmen in civilian life or who were army regulars with a special talent soon got the attention of their officers. The Germans were the first to use snipers in a systematic way. They were given camouflage, telescopic sights, and small metal shields with loopholes, but these shields soon proved a burden and were often disposed of by the men. Snipers were generally free of sentry and fatigue duty, and German snipers did not move with their units but stayed in the same sector for months on end, thereby becoming intimately familiar with the terrain.

Snipers on both sides often worked in pairs, with one man acting as a spotter and the other shooting. Snipers rarely stayed in the same place for long, instead moving around after a few shots and finding another vantage point, which kept them from becoming targets of sniper fire themselves. They also fired from craters or ruined buildings in No Man's Land, and some created fake trees with bulletproof shielding inside the trunks to hide inside. The Germans even tried flying kites with British writing on it so that when some foolish soldier popped his head above the parapet to try and read the words, he'd end up getting shot.

An Australian sniper team in a trench in 1915

Basic caution reduced the chance of being hit by a sniper, but getting rid of them proved difficult. One method was to have a few men watching a suspected sniper's nest while another man poked up a helmet on the end of a stick. If the sniper took the bait, he'd get several shots in his direction. More troublesome snipers could even attract a focused artillery barrage, and the lack of foresight can be seen in the fact that the men were not equipped with metal helmets to protect them when looking or firing over the parapet of a trench. Furthermore, artillery was provided with only a relatively small number of high-explosive shells. Instead, shrapnel shells were the most common type sent to the front, and they proved to have little effect against barbed wire (also in short supply in the opening months of the war) or against men hiding in entrenched positions.

The Germans were particularly good at building trenches and defensive positions, and when they had pulled back after the initial fighting in the early months of the war, they chose the best sites for their defensive lines. They also understood that in this war, once soldiers had dug in, the defense had the upper hand.

The Legacy of the Battle

In late August 1914, the Schlieffen Plan appeared to have a good chance of working, and it had achieved most of its objectives within the timetable, but there was still little margin for error, the German supply lines became stretched too thin, and the Germans did not know the landscape. The French, on the other hand, were fighting for survival and for their beloved capital, and of course, as the Allies retreated, their supply lines shortened.

The Schlieffen Plan had been carefully devised nearly a decade before World War I, but it had a fatal flaw from the very beginning, and that was its lack of reliance on the kind of communications that would be necessary in a modern war. The commanders in the field had trouble communicating with each other, especially across wide fronts, and these commanders had trouble communicating with Moltke, who remained stationed hundreds of miles away. Radio communications were not yet secure at that time, so the enemy was able to monitor messages. Besides, a complex operation such as that called for in the Schlieffen Plan needed to have excellent real-time communication, which the Germans quite clearly did not have. Even in the middle of the war, carrier pigeons remained a preferred method of sending messages.

It is quite clear that if the Allies could identify a gap with their air reconnaissance photography, the Germans should have done so as well, but German air reconnaissance was not nearly as good as that of the French. The French had a fully developed photographic reconnaissance air corps with several squadrons, and this ability not only helped turn the tide of battle, it provided the impetus for the operations at the beginning of the battle.

Finally, it's crucial to note that the Schlieffen Plan was also inflexible, which made it all but impossible to revise when events did not go as planned. As Holger Herwick put it, "The Germans gambled all on a brilliant operational concept. It was a single roll of the dice. There was no fallback, no Plan B."15

Trench warfare became Plan B, and while the Germans were very good at building trenches and establishing impenetrable defensive positions, a reliance on trench warfare not been thought

---

15 Herwick, Holger. Quoted by Hanc, John. "Fleet Taxis Did Not Really Save Paris Germans During World War I." Smithsonian.Com, JULY 24, 2014, https://www.smithsonianmag.com/history/fleet-taxis-did-not-really-save-paris-germans-during-world-war-i-180952140/#pzi1TZr2U4KdFJJR.99.

through as a coherent plan.

Of course, the ultimate failure of the Schlieffen Plan and the eventual German defeat in the war led to a search for scapegoats. The Germans needed to follow the Schlieffen Plan once they committed to it, so Moltke has been criticized for being indecisive, especially in failing to dissuade Rupprecht from the fateful attack. Of course, it's believed Kaiser Wilhelm II put pressure on Moltke in that instance, and that Moltke caved in and let the younger prince have his way.

Others note that General von Kluck of the 1st Army disobeyed direct orders to move closer to the 2nd Army and instead went after the French 6th Army, seemingly in a quest for glory. This was a major reason for the German withdrawal, and General French asserted, "The fact probably is that von Kluck and his Staff never really liked the role which was forced upon them by the Great General Staff, and they undertook their part in the battle with wavering minds and with their heads half turned round."[16]

Finally, there is the argument that the attack was under-powered from the beginning. Holmes concluded, "Moltke followed the trajectory of the Schlieffen Plan, but only up to the point where it was painfully obvious he would have needed the army of the Schlieffen Plan to proceed any further along these lines. Lacking the strength and support to advance across the lower Seine, his right wing became a positive liability, caught in an exposed position to the east of fortress Paris."[17]

Morale and fatigue were also factors that had not been taken into account enough. While the Germans were understandably exhausted, the French surprised the Germans with their ability to recover after the Great Retreat. In conjunction with that, most German soldiers and commanders in early September thought they had already practically won the campaign, and that it was only a matter of time before the French gave in. As a result of constant fighting and advancing, they were exhausted and overextended physically and emotionally, and when they realized the French and British were not beaten, it had a devastating effect on their own morale. General von Kluck gave this reason for the German withdrawal at the Marne: "The reason that transcends all others was the extraordinary and peculiar aptitude of the French soldier to recover quickly. ...that men will let themselves be killed where they stand, that is well-known and counted on in every plan of battle. But that men who have retreated for ten days, sleeping on the ground and half dead with fatigue, should be able to take up their rifles and attack when the bugle sounds, is a thing upon which we never counted. It was a possibility not studied in our war academy."[18]

While the specific actions each army and general took are clear, the reasons that Germany

---

[16] French, 1914.
[17] Holmes, T. M. (April 2014). "Absolute Numbers: The Schlieffen Plan as a Critique of German Strategy in 1914". War in History. Thousand Oaks, CA: Sage. 21 (2), p. 211.
[18] Tuchman 1962, p. 519.

withdrew when victory seemed within reach remain unclear. An official German inquiry and report about the war entitled *Das Marnedrama, 1914 (Drama of the Marne, 1914)* claimed that "the German army had retreated from its already won victory."19

General French, naturally, had a different take. He acknowledged the Allies did not know about the Schlieffen Plan, and because of this they had trouble understanding the strategies and movements of the German armies. French wrote the following:

> "Many different views have been put forward regarding the initial foundation upon which the Germans built up their strategic scheme for the invasion of France.
>
> "In the preparation of the German Army for this supreme moment not a chance had been thrown away. In man power, armament, training, and equipment; in the instruction of leaders and officers; on the choice of commanders and every other element which makes for efficiency in an army, the most laborious thought and care had been expended.
>
> "Splendidly, however, as the Allied Armies fought, skillfully as each of the various corps and armies which were engaged supported one another; it was the Germans themselves who deliberately threw away whatever chance they ever had of securing a decisive victory. We have seen that ... late as the morning of September 6th, Joffre and I were still so certain that the German thrust was in full career..."20

Despite their disadvantages, the Allies, who never wanted the war and did not have concrete plans in the summer of 1914, adeptly took advantage of the situation as events unfolded and successfully improvised as the German invasion went on. As a result, they eventually emerged victorious at the Marne and saved Paris in the process.

Pictures of the Battle

"4th Bn Royal Fusiliers 22 August 1914" 4th_Bn_Royal_Fusiliers_22_August_1914.jpg, Commons.wikimedia.org, August 22, 1914, https://commons.wikimedia.org/wiki/File:4th_Bn_Royal_Fusiliers_22_August_1914.jpg. Accessed 4/21/2019.

"Alfred von Schlieffen 1906." Alfred von Schlieffen 1906.jpg. Commons.wikimedia.org, Photo studio E. Bieber, 1906, https://en.wikipedia.org/wiki/File:Alfred_von_Schlieffen_1906.jpg. Accessed date?

---

19 Bose, Thilo von. *Das Marnedrama, 1914 (Drama of the Marne, 1914).* Monograph. Axis History Forum, (https://forum.axishistory.com), Oldenburg Germany, 1928,
20 French, 1914, Chapter VI.

"Battle of the Marne - Map" Battle_of_the_Marne_-_Map (1)A.jpg. Commons.wikimedia.org, The Department of History at the United States Military Academy, www.dean.usma.edu, 1938, https://commons.wikimedia.org/wiki/File:Battle_of_the_Marne_-_Map.jpg. Accessed date?

"British Field Marshal, Sir John French, Commander in Chief of the British Army from 1914-15." Field Marshal Sir John French 2.jpg. Commons.wikimedia.org, Hainer, Paris, https://commons.wikimedia.org/wiki/File:Field_Marshal_Sir_John_French_2.jpg Accessed date?

" 'Ce ciel est notre azur ce champ est notre terre! Cette Lorraine et cette Alsace, c'est á nous!' Victor Hugo" 3f03941v.jpg. Library of Congress Prints and Photographs Division Washington, D.C., 1918, http://www.loc.gov/pictures/item/99613754/. Accessed 4/21/2019.

"French general Joseph Gallieni (1849-1916)" Joseph Gallieni 01.jpg. Commons.wikimedia.org, George Grantham Bain Collection (Library of Congress), https://commons.wikimedia.org/wiki/File:Joseph_Gallieni_01.jpg. Accessed 4/21/2019.

"German Trenches on the Aisne." German trenches on the aisne.jpg. Commons.wikimedia.org, Library of Congress, Bain News Service, 1914, https://commons.wikimedia.org/wiki/File:German_trenches_on_the_aisne.jpg. Accessed 4/21/2019.

"Infanterie-française-rol" Infanterie-française-rol.jpg Commons.wikimedia.org, Bibliothèque nationale de France, 1914, https://commons.wikimedia.org/wiki/File:Infanterie-fran%C3%A7aise-rol.jpg. Accessed 4/21/2019.

"Les mobilisés parisiens devant la gare de l'Est le 2 août 1914." Les_mobilisés_parisiens_devant_la_gare_de_l'Est_le_2_août_1914.jpeg. Commons.wikimedia.org, Bibliothèque nationale de France, August 2, 1914, https://commons.wikimedia.org/wiki/File:Les_mobilis%C3%A9s_parisiens_devant_la_gare_de_l%27Est_le_2_ao%C3%BBt_1914.jpeg. Accessed 4/21/2019.

"Niemiecka pocztówka przedstawiajaca bombardowanie Warszawy w 1914." Der Kampf um Warschau postcard.jpg. Commons.wikimedia.org, Neue Photographische Gesellschaft Berlin, Bowman Gray Collection, 1914, https://commons.wikimedia.org/wiki/File:Der_Kampf_um_Warschau_postcard.jpg. Accessed 4/21/2019.

"Photo portrait of Gen Joffre (darker)." Photo portrait of Gen Joffre (darker).jpg. Commons.wikimedia.org, https://commons.wikimedia.org/wiki/File:Photo_portrait_of_Gen_Joffre_(darker).jpg. Accessed date?

"Race to the Sea 1914" Race to the Sea 1914.png. Commons.wikimedia.org, The Department of History at the United States Military Academy, www.dean.usma.edu, 1938, https://en.wikipedia.org/wiki/File:Race_to_the_Sea_1914.png. Accessed 4/21/2019.

"The Road To War Q81806." The_Road_To_War_Q81806.jpg. Commons.wikimedia.org, Imperial War Museums, Pre-1914, https://commons.wikimedia.org/wiki/File:The_Road_To_War_Q81806.jpg. Accessed 4/21/2019.

"Schlieffen Plan." Schlieffen_Plan.jpg. Commons.wikimedia.org, The Department of History at the United States Military Academy, www.dean.usma.edu, 1938, https://commons.wikimedia.org/wiki/File:Schlieffen_Plan.jpg. Accessed 4/21/2019.

"Taxi de la Marne, Musée de l'Armée" Taxi_de_la_Marne,_Musée_de_l'Armée-IMG_0987.jpg. Commons.wikimedia.org, Musée de l'Armée, Paris (Rama), 2006, https://commons.wikimedia.org/wiki/File:Taxi_de_la_Marne,_Mus%C3%A9e_de_l%27Arm%C3%A9e-IMG_0987.jpg. Accessed 4/21/2019.

"The Western Front, 1914" The_Western_Front,_1914_Q53452.jpg. Commons.wikimedia.org, Imperial War Museums, 1914, https://commons.wikimedia.org/wiki/File:The_Western_Front,_1914_Q53452.jpg. Accessed 4/21/2019.

.

Online Resources

Other World War I titles by Charles River Editors

Other titles about the Somme on Amazon

Bibliography

"Abandonment of Paris." WWI Document Archive > 1914 Documents > Abandonment of Paris, 1914, https://wwi.lib.byu.edu/index.php/Abandonment_of_Paris. Accessed 4/21/2019.

Allwood, Greg. "Deliverance On The Marne." Forces.Net, 5th September 2017, https://www.forces.net/news/deliverance-marne. Accessed 4/21/2019.

Baron Beyens (Belgian Minister at Berlin). "Speech in the Reichstag by the Imperial Chancellor on the violation of Belgian neutrality." The Belgian Grey Book, August 4, 1914, https://wwi.lib.byu.edu/index.php/The_Belgian_Grey_Book. Accessed 4/21/2019.

Barrès, Maurice. *The Faith of France*. Paris, Houghton Mifflin & Company, 1918.

Bose, Thilo von. *Das Marnedrama, 1914* (*Drama of the Marne, 1914*). Monograph. Axis History Forum, (https://forum.axishistory.com), Oldenburg Germany, 1928. Accessed 4/21/2019.

Churchill, Sir Winston. *The World Crisis*, 1911–1918, Free Press, 2005, ISBN 0 7432 8343 0, p. 168.

Churchill, Sir Winston. *The World Crisis, Volume V*. Bloomsbury Academic; New edition (March 26, 2015).

Fierro, Alfred. *Historical dictionary of Paris* (1998).

French, Field-Marshal John. *1914*. London, Constable And Company Ltd., 1919.

Grey, Sir Edward (3rd Baronet). "Sir Edward Grey, 3rd Baronet, British Statesman." Encyclopædia Britannica, www.britannica.com, https://www.britannica.com/biography/Sir-Edward-Grey-3rd-Baronet. Accessed 4/21/2019.

Herwick, Holger. Quoted by Hanc, John. "A Fleet of Taxis Did Not Really Save Paris From the Germans During World War I." Smithsonian.Com, JULY 24, 2014, https://www.smithsonianmag.com/history/fleet-taxis-did-not-really-save-paris-germans-during-world-war-i-180952140/#pzi1TZr2U4KdFJJR.99. Accessed 4/21/2019.

Holmes, T. M. (April 2014). "Absolute Numbers: The Schlieffen Plan as a Critique of German Strategy in 1914". War in History. Thousand Oaks, CA: Sage. 21 (2). ISSN 0968-3445.

Klein, Christopher. "The First Battle of the Marne." History.Com, Sept 5, 2014, https://www.history.com/news/the-first-battle-of-the-marne-100-years-ago. Accessed 4/21/2019.

Lomas, David. *Mons 1914: The BEF's Tactical Triumph*. Bloomsbury USA, 09/15/1997.

Lucas, Jon. "10 Deadliest Days on WWI's Western Front". Toptenz.Net, https://www.toptenz.net/10-deadliest-days-wwis-western-front.php. Accessed 4/21/2019.

Recouly Raymond. *Foch: Le Vainqueur de la Guerre* [*Foch: The victor of the war*]. Paris, France: Hachette, 1919.

Statement by General Joseph Joffre, 5th September, 1914. Spartacus-Educational.Com, https://spartacus-educational.com/U3Ahistory27.htm. Accessed 4/21/2019.

Trouillard, Stéphanie (August 22, 2014). "August 22, 1914: The bloodiest day in French military history". France 24, 22/08/2014, https://www.france24.com/en/20140822-august-22-1914-battle-frontiers-bloodiest-day-french-military-history. Accessed 4/21/2019.

Tuchman, Barbara Wertheim. *The Guns of August*. Ballantine Books, 1962.

Free Books by Charles River Editors

We have brand new titles available for free most days of the week. To see which of our titles are currently free, click on this link.

Discounted Books by Charles River Editors

We have titles at a discount price of just 99 cents everyday. To see which of our titles are currently 99 cents, click on this link.

Printed in Great Britain
by Amazon